The Cosmic Philosophy Of The Middle Ages

Viktor Rydberg

I.

THE COSMIC PHILOSOPHY OF THE MIDDLE AGES, AND ITS HISTORICAL DEVELOPMENT.

INTRODUCTORY.

It was the belief of Europe during the Middle Ages, that our globe was the centre of the universe.

The earth, itself fixed and immovable, was encompassed by ten heavens successively encircling one another, and all of these except the highest in constant rotation about their centre.

This highest and immovable heaven, enveloping all the others and constituting the boundary between created things and the void, infinite space beyond, is the Empyrean, the heaven of fire, named also by the Platonizing philosophers the world of archetypes. Here "in a light which no one can enter," God in triune majesty is sitting on his throne, while the tones of harmony from the nine

revolving heavens beneath ascend to him,
like a hymn of glory from the universe
to its Creator.

Next in order below the Empyrean is the
heaven of crystal, or the sphere of the *first
movable* (*primum mobile*). Beneath this re-
volves the heaven of fixed stars, which, formed
from the most subtile elements in the universe, are devoid of weight. If now an angel
were imagined to descend from this heaven
straight to earth,—the centre, where the
coarsest particles of creation are collected,—
he would still sink through seven vaulted
spaces, which form the planetary world. In
the first of these remaining heavens is found
the planet Saturn, in the second Jupiter,
in the third Mars; to the fourth and middle
heaven belongs the Sun, queen of the planets,
while in the remaining three are the paths
of Venus, Mercury, and finally the moon,
measuring time with its waning and increasing disk. Beneath this heaven of the moon
is the enveloping atmosphere of the earth,
and earth itself with its lands and seas.

There are four prime elements in the structure of the universe: fire, air, water and earth.
Every thing existing in the material world is
a peculiar compound of these elements, and
possesses as such an energy of its own; but
matter in itself is devoid of quality and force.
All power is spiritual, and flows from a spiritual source,—from God, and is communicated
to the earth and the heavens above the earth
and all things in them, by spiritual agents,
personal but bodiless. These beings fill the
universe. Even the prime elements derive
their energy from them. They are called intelligences or angels; and the *primum mobile*
as well as the heaven of fixed stars is held
in motion by them. The planets are guided
in their orbits by angels. " All the energies
of plants, metals, stones and all other objects,
are derived from those intelligences whom
God has ordained to be the guardians and
leaders of his works."* " God, as the source
and end of all power, lends the seal of ideas

---

* Henricus Cornelius Agrippa ab Nettesheim: "De occulta
Philosophia."—I., xiii.

to his ministering spirits, who, faithfully executing his divine will, stamp with a vital energy all things committed to their care."[*]

No inevitable causation is admitted. Every thing is produced by the will of God, and upheld by it. The laws of nature are nothing but the precepts in accordance with which the angels execute their charge. They obey from love and fear; but should they in a refractory spirit transgress the given commandments, or cease their activity, which they have the power to do, then the order of nature would be changed, and the great mechanism of the universe fall asunder, unless God saw fit to interpose. " Sometimes God suspends their agency, and is himself the immediate actor everywhere; or he gives unusual commandments to his angels, and then their operations are called miracles."[†]

A knowledge of the nature of things is consequently in the main a knowledge of the

---

[*] Henricus Cornelius Agrippa ab Nettesheim : 'De occulta Philosophia."—I., xiii.

[†] *Ibidem.*

angels. Their innumerable hosts form nine choirs or orders, divided into three hierarchies, corresponding to the three worlds: the empyreal, that of the revolving heavens, and the terrestrial. The orders of Seraphim, Cherubim and Thrones which constitute the first hierarchy, are nearest God. They surround his throne like a train of attendants, rejoice in the light of his countenance, feel the abundant inspiration of his wisdom, love and power, and chant eternal praises to his glory. The order of the Thrones, which is the lowest in this empyreal hierarchy, proclaims God's will to the middle hierarchy, to which is given the rule of the movable heavens. It is the order of Dominion which thus receives the commands of God; that of Power, which guides the stars and planets in their orbits, and brings to pass all other celestial phenomena, carries them into execution, while a third of Empire wards off every thing which could interfere with their accomplishment. The third and lowest hierarchy, embracing the orders of Principalities, Archangels and Angels, holds supremacy over terrestrial things. Principalities, as the name implies, are the guardian spirits of nations and kingdoms; Archangels protect religion, and bear the prayers of saints on high to the throne of God; Angels, finally, have the care of every mortal, and impart to beasts, plants, stones and metals their peculiar nature. Together these hierarchies and orders form a continuous chain of intermingling activities, and thus the structure of the universe resembles a Jacob's ladder, upon which

"Celestial powers, mounting and descending,
  Their golden buckets ceaseless interchange."

All terrestrial things are images of the ce lestial; and all celestial have their archetypes in the Empyrean. Things on earth are composed of the coarsest of all matter; things in the surrounding heavens of a finer substance, accessible to the influence of intelligences. Archetypes are immaterial; and as such may be filled without resistance with spiritual forces, and give of their plenitude to

their corresponding effigies in the worlds of
stars and planets. These again through their
rays send forth of the abundance of their
power to those objects on earth by which
they are represented. Every thing on earth
is consequently not only under the guidance
of its own angel, but also under the influence
of stars, planets, and archetypes. The universe is a vast lyre whose strings, struck no
matter where, are sure to vibrate throughout
their length.

It was for man that God called forth the
four elements from nothing by his fiat, and it
was for man that he fashioned this wonderful
earth from those elements in six days. Man
is the crown of creation, its master-piece, and
within the narrow limits of his nature an epit-
ome of all things existing,—a microcosm, and
the image of the supreme God himself.

But since man, as a microcosm, must partake also of the coarsest matter, his dwelling-place could not be within the Empyrean,
but must be fixed on earth. In order that
it might be worthy to receive him, it was

adorned with all the beauty of a paradise, and angels gazed from heaven with delight upon its vales and mountains, its lakes and groves, which in changing lights and shadows shone now with the purple of morning, now with the gold of the sun, and again with the silver of the moon. And this place of habitation explains symbolically by its very position the destiny of man and his place in the kingdom of God; for wherever he wanders, the zenith still lingers over his head, and all the revolving heavens have his habitation for their centre. The dance of the stars is but a fête in honor of him, the sun and moon exist but to shine upon his pathway and fill his heart with gladness.

The first human beings lived in this their paradise in a state of highest happiness. Their will was undepraved; their understanding filled with the immediate light of intuition. Often when the angel of the sun sank with his gleaming orb towards the horizon and " day was growing cool," God himself descended from his Empyrean to wander under the lovely trees of paradise, in the company of his favored ones.

The world was an unbroken harmony. There was, to be sure, a contrast between spirit and matter, but as yet none between good and evil. It was not long to remain thus.

Lucifer, that is the Light-bringer, or Morning Star, was the highest of all angels, the prince of seraphim, the favorite of the Creator, and in purity, majesty and power inferior only to the Holy Trinity. Pride and envy took possession, it is not known how, of this mighty spirit. He conceived the plan of overthrowing the power of God, and seating himself upon the throne of Omnipotence. Angels of all orders were won over to his treason. At the first beck of the reckless spirit numberless intelligences from the lower heavens and from earth assailed the Empyrean and joined themselves to the rebellious seraphim, cherubim and thrones who had flocked to the standard of revolt. In heaven raged a mighty contest, the vicissitudes of which are covered by the veil of mystery. St. John, however, in his Book of Revelation, lifts a single fold of it, and shows us Michael at the head of the legions of God battling against Lucifer. The contest ended with the overthrow of the rebel and his followers. The beautiful Morning Star fell from heaven.* Christ beheld the once faithful seraph hurled from its ramparts like a thunderbolt from the clouds.†

The conquered was not annihilated. Calm in the consciousness of omnipotence, God inscrutably determined that Lucifer, changed by his rebellion into a spirit wholly evil, should enjoy liberty of action within certain limits. The activity of the fallen spirit consists in desperate and incessant warfare against God; and he gains in the beginning a victory of immeasurable consequence. He tempts man, and brings him under his dominion.

* This passage, directed against the ruler of Assyria, was already interpreted by the early fathers as having reference to Satan. Thus Lucifer, the Latin translation for Morning Star, came to be a name for the prince of darkness.

† Luke x. 18.

Humanity, as well as the beautiful earth which is its abode, is under the curse of God.

The world is no longer an unbroken harmony, a moral unity. It is divided forever into two antagonistic kingdoms, those of Good and Evil. That God so wills, and permits the inevitable consequences, is confirmed by an immediate change in the structure of the universe. Death is sent forth commissioned to destroy all life. Hell opens its jaws in the once peaceful realms of earth's bosom, and is filled with a fire which burns every thing, but consumes nothing.

The battle-field is the whole creation except the spaces of the Empyrean; for into its pure domain nothing corrupt can enter. Lucifer still adheres to his claims upon its throne, and in every thing seeks to imitate God. The fallen seraphim, cherubim and thrones constitute his princely retinue and his council of war. The rebel intelligences of the middle hierarchy, now transformed into demons, still love to rove among the same stars and planets which were once confided to their care, and war against the good angels who now guide the movements of the heavens. Other demons float upon the atmosphere, causing storm and thunder, hail and snow, drouth and awful omens (whence it is said the devil is a prince who controls the weather). Others again fill the earth; its seas, lakes, fountains and rivers; its woods, groves, meadows and mountains. They pervade the elements; they are everywhere.

Man, the chief occasion of the strife, is in a sad condition. The bodily pains and sufferings which the earth since its curse heaps upon the path that successive generations, all partakers of Adam's sin, must tread, are as nothing compared with the perils which on all sides assail and threaten their immortal souls. And how can these dangers be averted? Each mortal is indeed followed from his birth by a guardian angel; but how can his promptings be distinguished from those that issue from the thousand hidden agents of the Evil. Lucifer can transform himself into an angel of light, his demons can entice with a voice which counterfeits that of God and conscience. Man's will has no power to resist these temptations; it is depraved by the fall. Reason gives no guidance; darkened on account of man's apostasy, it degenerates, if left to itself, into a Satanic instrument of heresy and error. Feeling is in subjection to matter, which, already from the beginning opposed to spirit, shares the curse. Is it then to be wondered at that the career of man, beginning with conception in a sinful womb, has for its end, behind the portals of death, the eternal torments of a hell? All these myriads of souls created by God and clothed in garments of clay,—all these microcosms, each of which is a master-piece, the glory of creation, a being of infinite value, form, link by link, a chain extending from that nothingness out of which God has created them, to that abyss in which, after a brief life on earth, they must be tormented through countless ages, despairing and cursing their Creator.

Lucifer triumphs. His kingdom increases; but the poor mortal has no right to complain. The vessel must not blame the potter. When man looks into his own heart he discovers a sinfulness and depravity as infinite as are his punishments. However severe the law of the universe appears, it still bears the impress of divine justice.

It is, therefore, but an act of pure grace, when God determines the salvation of mankind. The Church, prepared for by the election of the Jewish people, and founded by Jesus Christ the Son of God, who offered himself for crucifixion to atone for the sins of men, has grown up and disseminated its influences throughout regions where once demons, the gods of the heathen, possessed temples, idols and altars. The Church is the magic circle within which alone is salvation possible (*Extra ecclesiam nullus salus*). Within her walls the Son of God offers himself daily as a sacrifice for the transgressions of humanity; the Communion wine is by a miracle changed into his blood, and the bread into his flesh, which, eaten by the members of the Church, promote their growth in holiness and their power of resistance to the Tempter. The Church is one body, animated by the Holy Spirit of God; and thus one member compensated by surplus of virtue for the deficiencies of another. Holy men, resigning all sensual delights, and devoting their lives to the practice of penance and severities, the contemplation of spiritual things, and doing good, accumulate thereby a wealth of supererogatory works, which, deposited in the treasury of the Church, enables her to compound for the sins of less self-denying members. With liberal hand she grants remission of sins not to the living merely, but also to the dead. Thus the race of men may breathe more freely, and the multitude attach themselves again to the transient joys and pleasures of a wretched life on earth; and when a mortal plucks the flowers of pleasure which bloom in this vale of sorrows, he need not fear so much its hidden poison, for the remedy is near at hand. The knight in the

castle yonder on the summit of the crag, or
the burgher beneath him in the valley, may
without scruple take a wife, rear children and
live in conviviality according to his means;
the happy student may sing and realize his
" *Gaudeamus igitur* "; the undaunted soldier
may seek a recompense for the hardships of
his campaign by a merry life in taverns and
in women's company; even the followers of
Mary Magdalene, sinning in expectation of
grace, may obtain at the feet of the Church
the same absolution which was given to their
model at the feet of Jesus, provided only
that, grateful for the mercy of Christ, who
has made them members of his Church, they
venerate it as their mother, partake of its
sacraments, and seek its aid. The continually increasing number of cloisters, the homes
of rigorous self-denial, uninterrupted penance,
and mysterious contemplation, is a guarantee
of the inexhaustibleness of those works of
supererogation which the Church possesses.
In these cloisters young maidens, who have
consecrated themselves to Christ after a spirit-

ual embrace for which the most intense impulses of their nature have been suppressed, yearn away their lives. Here in prayer and toil the pious recluse spends his days and nights. Those men also who, going forth barefooted, covered with coarse mantles, and wearing ropes about their waists, devote themselves like the apostles to poverty and the preaching of the gospel, who receive charity at the door of the layman, giving him in exchange the food of the word of God,— these all issue from the same cloisters.

Thus is the Church a mole against the tide of Sin. The Christian has some reason to exclaim: "O hell, where is thy victory?" for although the place of torment is continually filled with lost spirits, there are thousands upon thousands of ransomed souls that wing their flight to the Empyrean,—whether immediately or by the way of Purgatory. First among the beatified who mingling with angels surround the throne of God, are those called saints. Their intercession is more efficacious even than that of seraphim, and their

power in the contest against the demons sur-
passes that of cherubim. Therefore kingdoms, communities, orders, corporations and
guilds, yea, even lawless and disreputable
professions (so needing grace and intercession more than others) have their patron
saints. The individual finally is protected by
the saint in whose name he has been baptized.

The Church is the kingdom of God on
earth; her ecclesiastical hierarchy is an image of the heavenly; her highest ruler, the
Pope, is God's vicar. Her destiny, which is
extension over the whole earth so as to include
all lands and nations within her magic circle,
could not be realized unless she possessed
the power to command the kings and armies
of Christendom. It is evident, moreover, that
spiritual power is above secular: the former
protects the soul, the latter the body only.
They stand related to one another as spirit is
related to matter. Therefore it must be the
Pope who shall invest with the highest secular dignity,—that of the Roman Cæsars. He
is the feudal lord of the emperors, as the em-

peror is, or should be, of the kings, dukes and free cities. Were it not thus,—if the various rulers were independent of the guardians of religion,—then woe to the great mass of their subjects! To be sure these multitudes are placed on earth to be disciplined by humanity and obedience; they have indeed no rights upon which they may insist, since they stand outside the pale of freedom; but, on the other hand, the oppression exercised upon them would have no limit unless the Church, who is the common mother of all, reminded those in authority of their duty to love and cherish the lowly: indeed, all social order would crumble into dust, did not a higher power than that dependent upon the sword compel the stronger to fulfil those vows to protect the weaker which he made in the presence of the Holy Trinity. For the only existing rights are those of privilege and investiture, founded absolutely upon sealed stipulations.

According to the doctrines of the Church, which are the only key to salvation, man has received as a gift what he never could have attained by science,—a knowledge of the highest truths. Possessed of this knowledge he must no longer allow himself to be tempted by the devil to engage in efforts to penetrate the mysteries of the universe with nothing to aid him but his darkened intellect; for such attempts generally end in error and apostasy. Still the allurement is strong because the highest truths, when clothed in the garb of human conceptions, sometimes appear self-contradictory and absurd. They must therefore be submitted, not to the decisions of reason, but the arbitration of faith. Faith alone is able to penetrate and apprehend them. The doctrines which the Church, assisted by the Holy Spirit, promulgates, since they alone are true, offer to the believing investigator a mine of infinite treasures. There is consequently possible within the Church a system of philosophy, provided that its processes, always postulating the infallibility of the dogmas, be confined to devout analysis and humble contemplation of religious tenets. For such a purpose the adherent of the scholastic philosophy may employ the Aristotelian dialectics as he chooses, and wield the lever of syllogism at his pleasure. Even within the pale of orthodoxy there may arise many an *if* and *but*, many a *pro* and *contra*. The scholastic reasoner has to prove but the most probable; the infallible Pope and his synods sanction the true deductions and refute the errors which, when recanted, are forgiven. It is best for the inquirer to found his researches on the propositions laid down by the early fathers of the Church; for thus succeeding generations will build on foundations laid for them by their predecessors long before. Inasmuch as they all follow the same dialectic method of analysis and synthesis, so that the whole subject is pervaded and its masses grouped into architectural order by these processes, there is reared on the basis of the dogma a philosophical superstructure, resembling those cupolas with which the skilful masters of masonry amaze our eyes.

The world grows worse. The Church can pardon sin, but can not hinder its increase. Every generation inherits from the preceding a burden of evil dispositions, habits and examples, which it lays in its turn still heavier on the shoulders of posterity. Every son has better reason for sighing than his father. "Happy those who died ere beholding the light of day! who tasted death ere the experience of life!"* The hosts of Satan assail the Church on every side. From his tower the watchman of Zion looks out over the world, and beholds the billows of history, now lashed fiercely by the demons, roll against the rock upon which Christ has built his temple. With great difficulty the cross-adorned hosts of Europe repel the invasion of the Saracens, whose coming has been prefigured by pestilences and portents. The emblem of the Church is an ark tossed about on a stormy sea amid a tempest of

---

* "De Contemptu Mundi sive de Miseria Humanæ Conditionis," a little book written about 1200, by the afterwards Pope Innocent III.

rain and lightning. History is a spiritual comedy, enacted on a stage of which the broad foreground, like that of the mysteries, is a *theatrum diabolorum;* while in the narrow background the Church of God, like a beleaguered citadel, points its pinnacles above the turmoil towards the gloomy sky, from which its defenders expect Jesus and his angels to come to their relief.

But before this relief arrives, iniquity shall have reached its height. It is at work already within the sacred precincts of the Church itself. It is with greater difficulty that God's vicar subdues the inner than the outer enemies. On the one hand many a man believes that he has found in his own reason and conscience leading truths, which he arrays, without any authority outside of himself, against those commandments which have come from above, and the divine origin of which is confirmed by the faith of a hundred generations. He places himself in an attitude of opposition to the common faith. Thus originate the heresies,—those cancers on the body of the congregation which must be cured by the iron, when salves will not restore, and by fire when the iron is ineffective. On the other hand men are so overpowered by their passions that they abandon the God who rebukes them, and become the bondsmen of another god who shows them favor. Pride, fettered by obscure descent, and keen appetite for pleasure chained from gratification by penury and privation, shake their shackles in despair, and finally call the Morning Star of old to their assistance. The archfiend promises pleasures without stint, and power without limitation. The poor mortal for dread of the pains which afflict his body is urged on to his destruction. His body formed from the dust of the accursed earth, and always a centre of sensual desires, is abandoned by God a prey to the assaults of the devil. "Here somebody loses an eye, somebody there a hand; one falls into the fire and is burned to death, one into the water and is drowned; another climbs a ladder and breaks his neck, another again stumbles on the even ground and breaks a leg. All such

unforeseen accidents, occurring daily, are but
the devil's thumps and strokes which he inflicts
upon us from sheerest malice."*   Still more:
the demon is able to take possession so thor-
oughly of the human body that he becomes,
as it were, its second soul, moves its limbs,
utters blasphemies with its tongue at which
even their fiendish author can not but tremble.
But though the God-fearing man, like pious
Job, is benefited by such afflictions, and although prayer is a powerful refuge, still there
is a continually growing number of those who,
driven by cowardly dread of the might of the
Prince of Evil, seek their safety in a league
with him; so much the more as he lends them
a partial control of the elements, and thus a
means of employment and of doing harm to
others.   Thus the dire pestilence of sorcery
multiplies its victims; and in the black hours
of midnight hundreds of thousands who bear
the name of Christian, on mountains and in

---

* The words of Luther, who, in addition to his dualistic
belief, was a genuine son of this same Middle Age, though
the destroyer of its autocratic faith.

deserts perform clandestine rites in honor of their Satanic master. Time ripens for the advent of Antichrist, for the Day of Judgment and the final conflagration.

In the flames of this last day the revolving heavens and the earth are destroyed. Motion, activity, strife, history,—all are at an end. The Empyrean and Hell alone remain, as the antipodal extremes of the former universe. This conflagration is not a universal purifier, annihilating what has no existence in itself.* It only separates forever the gold

---

* As such,—as perishable and unreal, are all evil things regarded by an unknown author in the Middle Ages. In his beautiful opuscule "Deutsche Theologie," he says among other things: "Now some one may ask, 'Since we must love every thing, must we also love sin?' The answer is, no; for when we say every thing, we only mean every thing that is good. Every thing that exists is good by virtue of its existence. The devil is good in so far as he exists. In this sense, there is nothing evil in existence. But it is a sin to wish, desire or love any thing else than God. Now all things are essentially in God, and more essentially in God than in themselves; therefore are they all good in their real essence."—The little work from which the above is quoted, is the expression of a deep and pious soul, struggling to master the dualism which fettered his age. It is remarkable that Luther was not more strongly influenced by its

from the dross. The kingdom of the devil continues to exist, and its prey is its own for evermore. But it exists thus only because an eternal existence means an eternal punishment for its ruler as well as for his subjects. From the new heavens and the new earth which the fiat of God has created to be the dwelling-place of those who have escaped destruction, these ransomed spirits perceive the gnashing of teeth and lamentation of their doomed brethren, and look down upon their tortures and misery, not with compassion but with joy, because they recognize in their punishment the vindication of divine justice; not with pain but delight, because the sight of their wretchedness doubles their own felicity. From the depths of that gulf of misery ascend without ceasing, to the Empyrean, cries of despair, blasphemies of defiance, and curses of rage, yet do they not disturb the hymns which saints and angels sing ever around the throne

spirit, although he confesses that "Next to the Bible and St. Augustine I have found no book from which I have learned more."

of God and of the Lamb; they only intensify the solemnity of the worship.*

Such in its chief features was the cosmic philosophy of the Middle Ages; not abstractly considered, but such as existed in reality during many centuries among Christian people, guiding their thoughts, imagination and feelings, and governing their actions. Remains of it are still apparent in the systems of existing sects, though incompatible with the new philosophy which the human mind has

---

* See the work "Summa Theologica" (supplementum ad tertiam partem, quæst. 94) by the most prominent and most influential among the theologians of the Middle Ages, Thomas Aquinas. It is there said: "Ut beatitudo sanctorum eis magis complaceat et de ea uberiores gratias Deo agant, datur eis ut pœnam impiorum perfecte videant . . Beati, qui erunt in gloria, nullam compassionem ad damnatos habebunt. . . Sancti de pœnis impiorum gaudebunt, considerando in eis divinæ justitiæ ordinem et suam liberationem de qua gaudebunt." —With this may be compared the following execrable effusion of another theologian: "Beati cœlites non tantum non cognatorum sed nec parentum sempiternis suppliciis ad ullam miserationem flectentur. Imo vero lætabuntur justi, cum viderint vindictam; manus lavabunt in sanguine peccatorum."

been laboring to unfold. Ever since the intellect of Christendom began to free itself in the sixteenth century from faith by authority, the influence of the old views upon the various forms which life takes on, has been gradually declining.

Many of those characteristics which so strangely contrast the state of society in the Middle Ages with the preceding Hellenic and the subsequent modern European civilizations, have their origin in different theories of the universe. It is not mere chance that we encounter, on the one hand, in the history of Greece, so many harmonious forms with repose and tranquil joy depicted in every lineament of their countenance, and on the other, in that of the Middle Ages, so many beings buried in deepest gloom or exalted in frenzied rapture, dripping with blood from self-inflicted wounds, or glowing with the fever of mystic emotion—not a mere chance that the former age loves those serene forms and immortalizes them in its heroic galleries, while the latter worships its eccentric figures and describes them in its legends as saintly models. It is not a mere accident that the art of Greece mirrors a beautiful humanity, while that of the Middle Ages loves to dwell upon monstrosities and throws itself between the extremes of awful earnestness and wild burlesque; not an accident only that the science of the Greek is rational—that he discovers the categories in Logic, and rears a most perfect structure of rigid demonstration in his Geometry, while the science of the Middle Ages on the contrary is *magic*,—is a doctrine of correspondencies, Astrology, Alchemy, and Sorcery.

To the Greek the universe was a harmonious unity. The law of reason, veiled under the name of fate, ruled the gods themselves. The variegated events of the myth lay far away in the distance; they did not even warp the imagination of the poet, when he occupied himself with them; still less the faith of the multitude, and least of all the investigations of the thinker. The uninterrupted sequence of events invited to contemplation, which could be indulged in the more readily, as no one pretended to have received as a gift a complete system of revealed truth, and the more freely, as no authority forced the individual to choose between such a system and perdition. In general no doubt was entertained concerning the ability of Reason to penetrate to the inner essence of things, since no knowledge of the fall of man, which annihilated this ability, had reached the Greeks. In regard to knowledge the Greek consequently built on evidence and inner authority. The same was the case in regard to morality. They were convinced that those impulses which promoted the happiness of domestic life, were good; and that those which did not counteract it were at least justified; and thus they enjoyed with moderation the gifts of nature, without suspicion that the bountiful giver was accursed. The ideal of wisdom which they had framed, was based on their inner experience, whether it had the joyous features of Epicurus, the severer lineaments of Zeno, or the mild and

resigned expression of Epictetus; and when
they exerted themselves to realize it in their
lives, they always proceeded upon the suppo-
sition that this would be possible by a daily
strengthening of the will. The exertion put
forth by the Greeks to attain to purity and
virtue was, as it were, a system of gymnas-
tics for developing the muscles of the brain.
The same power and self-confidence were dis-
played in these endeavors as in the palaestra.
Sighs and anguish were strangers to this kind
of reformatory effort. Yet was it not alto-
gether fruitless. The old adage that God
helps those who help themselves can be here
applied. That it developed great, powerful,
and noble natures was so undeniable that
even one of the Christian fathers, upon con-
sidering their achievements, began to doubt
if his way of attaining perfection was really
the only one, until he succeeded in convinc-
ing himself that "The virtues of the Gentiles
are shining vices." The harmonious personality of the Greek and the rationality of Grecian science depended on the unity, the har-

mony of their cosmic views—upon this, that
they conceived of the whole as a unity in its
diversity, not as an irreconcilable disunion
of two absolutely antagonistic principles.

If, on the contrary, the highest ruling power in nature is an arbitrary divine caprice, if
the world which lies open before mankind is
ruled by another's purely fortuitous decrees,
themselves interfered with continually by hostile influences from an infernal kingdom; if,
moreover, this struggle rages not merely in
the external world, but also in the very core
of human nature, vitiating her reason, feelings and will, so to employ them without
her agency as means to her exaltation or
perdition, then is there indeed no causality
to be sought for, and consequently no field
anywhere for scientific investigation. Were
there even any such thing as science, it would
lie far beyond the powers of man, since reason,
a mere plaything for demoniac powers, can
not be trusted. Neither has his personality
any longer its centre of gravity within itself.
Then is man in excessive need of such an in-

stitution of deliverance as the Church, which teaches him what the divine authority has arbitrarily decided to be good or evil; while the supernatural means of grace, the sacraments, afford him power of resisting evil, and absolve him from his failings. In this way external authority supplants the inner, which is torn up by the roots. That ideal of human perfection which is possible under such conditions, and which actually arises because the native activity of the mind constantly endeavors to bring all accepted notions into union, places itself on the doctrine of authority as its foundation, and accepts its supernatural character. That the ideal of the Middle Ages is ascetic and its science magical, is directly consequent upon its dualistic conception of the universe and of its peculiar nature.

The dualism of the Middle Ages was derived from Persia. It is the essential idea of the Zoroastrian doctrine, which finally, after a long struggle against the unitarian notions of the Greeks, penetrates the Occident and completely conquers it. This vic-

torious combat of the Orient against Europe
is the sum of history between Cyrus and
Constantine. The external events which fill
those centuries obtain their true significance
when within and behind them one perceives
the struggle between the two conflicting systems of ideas. Like concealed chess-play-
ers they move their unconscious champions
against each other on the board of history.

When Cyrus sends home the Jewish pris-
oners from the rivers of Babylon to the
mountains of Jerusalem, he gains for dualism that important flank-position on the Med-
iterranean the significance of which is shown
centuries after in the progress of the battle.
The " Adversary" (Satan) who sometimes
appears in the most recent portions of the
Old Testament, written under Persian influence, and plays a continually widening role
in the Rabbinical literature, is the Judaized
Ahriman; the demoniacs who in the time of
Christ abounded in Palestine testify that the
demon-belief of Persian dualism had pene-
trated into the imagination and feeling of the

Jews, and there borne fruit. By the side of this peaceful conquest the great war-drama between Greece and Persia is enacted. Although this is not recognizedly a religious war, it is nevertheless Ormuzd and Ahriman who are repelled at Marathon, Salamis and Platæa, it is the Grecian unitarianism which is saved in these battles to develop itself, for a season undisturbed, into a radiant and beautiful culture. As has been shown already, magic, and belief upon authority, are the necessary consequences of a dualistic religion; the restriction and annihilation of free personality are equally necessary consequences of belief by authority. Can any one regarding the conflict which raged on the field of Marathon, fail to recognize the clash of two spiritual opposites, two different systems of ideas, when he sees the bands of Greeks, drawn from their agorai (places for political discussion) and gymnasiums, advance cheerfully and garlanded, but without depreciating the danger, to meet the innumerable hosts of the Orient driven on by the scourge of their leaders? On the one side, a fully developed free personality, which has its origin in a harmonious conception of nature, on the other, blind submission to external force. On the one side, liberty, on the other, despotism. One may add by the help of a logical conclusion, though this may seem more removed,—on the one side rationality, on the other magic.

Strengthened thus by victory Europe goes to seek the enemy in his own country. Alexander conquers Asia. But the new Achilles is fettered in the chains of his own slave. For while Greek culture is spreading over the surface of the conquered countries, the Oriental spirit advances beneath it in a contrary direction. The waves of the two ideal currents are partly mingled. In the libraries of Alexandria and Pergamus the literatures of the Orient and of the Occident flow together; in their halls meet the sages of the East and West; in their doctrinal systems Zoroaster and Plato, fancy and speculation, magic and rationalism are blended in the

most extraordinary way. The victory of
Alexander was that of the warrior, and not
that of sober Aristotle's pupil. The Judaico-
Alexandrian philosophy blooms, and gnosti-
cism,—that monstrous bastard of specifically
different cosmical systems, is already begotten, when Christianity springs up in Palestine,
and unites itself with the Jewish dualism derived from Zoroaster, and thus proceeds to
conquer the world by the weapons of belief.

In the mean time Rome has extended and
established its empire. The nationalities included in it have been mingled together;
their various gods have been carried into the
same Pantheon; and their ideas have been
brought face to face. The universal empire,
to maintain its existence, has been forced to
centralize itself into a despotism of the Oriental type, the free forms of state have per-
ished, philosophical skepticism and eudemon-
ism have abolished among the cultured classes
the inherited notions of religion. All this,
with its accompaniments of moral depravity
and material necessity, have prepared the soil

of the Occident for receiving the seed of the new religion. Emptiness and misery make the difference between ideality and reality, between good and evil, all the more perceptible even to unitarian nations. Dualism thus prepared for in the realms of thought and feeling, spreads in Christian form with irresistible force over the Roman provinces. Innumerable masses of the poor and oppressed devote themselves to the " philosophy of the Barbarians and the Orient " (as a Greek thinker called Christianity) because they recognize in it their own experience of life, and have full assurance in their hope of relief.

The Hellenico-Roman paganism offers a fruitless resistance. The persecutions on the part of the state only hasten the spread of Christianity. What the state can not do, perhaps the Hellenic culture and philosophy may do. These, once mutually hostile, are reconciled in the face of common danger. The dying lamp of antiquity flares and brightens when pure hearts and profound minds, otherwise despising the myths as superstition, now grasp them as symbols of higher truths. Philosophy goes forth, in the form of Neoplatonism.

But Neoplatonism has . itself apostatized from the rational and unitarian. Plotinus and Ammonius Saccas try in vain to restore it. It only unwittingly helps its adversary, especially when, to gain the masses, it consents to compete with him in miracles. Jamblichus and others practice secret arts in order to outrival the Christian magi, and they glorify Pythagoras and Appollonius of Tyana as fit to rank with Jesus of Nazareth in miraculous gifts. By this they only contribute to the spread of magic and the principles of dualism. The current of Oriental notions proceeds all the more rapidly on its course of triumph.

Christian dualism already feels itself strong enough to battle not only against its declared enemies, but also those Occidental elements of culture which in its beginnings it had received into its bosom and which had procured its entrance among the more intelligent classes. It feels instinctively that even the school of thought which has sprung up within the Church is far too unitarian and rationalistic to be tolerated in the long run. Such men as Clemens of Alexandria and Origen, who are struck by what is external and imperishable in Christianity, and know how to separate this from its dualistic form, fight a tragical battle for the union of belief and thought. Admitting that Christ is all in all, the immediate power and wisdom of God, they nevertheless wish to save the Hellenic philosophy from the destruction which a fanaticism, revelling in the certainty and all-sufficiency of revelation, directs against every expression of an occidental culture, whether in national life, or art, or science. They point out that philosophy, if it can do nothing else that is good, can furnish rational weapons against those who assail faith, and that it can and ought to be the "real wall of defence about the vineyard." Their argument is without effect. Philosophy is of the devil: yea, everything true and good in life and doctrine which heathendom has possessed, is declared by one of the fathers to be the imposture of Satan (*ingenia diaboli quædam de divinis affectandis*); and faith is so far independent of thought that it is better to say "I believe *because* it is improbable, absurd, impossible." *   In vain the dying Clemens exclaims: "Even if philosophy were of the devil, Satan could deceive men only in the garb of an angel of light: he must allure men by the appearance of truth, by the intermixture of truth and falsehood; we ought therefore to seek and recognize the truth from whatever source it come. . . And even this gift to the pagans can have been theirs only by the will of God, and must consequently be included in the divine plan of educating humanity. . . If sin and disorder are attributable to the devil, how absurd to make him the author and giver of so good a thing as philosophy! . . . . God gave the Law to the Jews, and philosophy to the Gentiles,

* Tertullian.

only to prepare for the coming of Christ."
Such are the words that ring out the last
dying echo of Hellenic culture and humanity! It is not a mere accident that with
philosophy Clemens and Origen also sought
to save the unitarian principles in so far as
to reject the doctrine of eternal punishment
in hell, and maintain that the devil will finally become good, and God be all in all.
But such a view could not command atten-
tion at a time when Christianity, only because it was not sharply and consistently dualistic, felt itself endangered by that wholly
consistent and thorough-going dualism which
under the name of Manicheism once more
advanced against Europe from the Persian
border. Although Manicheism seemed to in-
cur defeat, nevertheless one of its former
adherents, Augustine, infused its spirit into
the Church. During the century which followed him the Germanic migration destroyed,
along with the last schools, the last vestiges
of Græco-Romaic culture. The Barbarians
were persuaded to receive baptism, often by

means of pomp and deceit; their divinities,
as formerly the denizens of Olympus, were
degraded to evil demons. Every thing an-
tecedent to their union with the Church or
disconnected with it,—the old experiences
and traditions of these converted nations,—
all was condemned and referred to the world
of evil. The dominion of Oriental dualism
in Europe was absolutely established, and
the long night of the Dark Ages had set in.
Six centuries separate Proclus, the last Neo-
platonican of any note, and Augustine the
last of the Fathers educated in philosophy,
from Anselm the founder of scholasticism!
Between them lies an expanse in which
Gregory the Great and Scotus Erigena are
almost the only stars, and these by no means
of the first magnitude. "There are deserts
in time, as well as space," says Bacon.

When again a feeble attempt at scientific
activity was possible, the monkish scholar
was happy enough to possess a few macu-
lated leaves of Aristotle, obtained, but not
directly, from the Arabs. Upon these leaves

he read with amazement and admiration the method for a logical investigation. It was, for the rest, Hermes Trismegistus, Dionysius Areopagita (the translation of Scotus Erigena), and other such mystical works from unknown hands, with here and there touches of Neoplatonism which had been inserted by the dreamy scholiast when in need of material for rounding out the cosmology, the principles of which he had found in the dogmas of the Church.

As a matter of course the Dark Ages could not perceive, still less admit, the intimate relation existing between its cosmic views and those of Zoroaster; but still a dim suspicion of it can be detected. The learned men of the Middle Ages ascribed to Zoroaster the founding of the magical sciences. Sprenger (author of Malleus Malificarum, of which fatal work hereafter), Remigius, Jean Bodin, Delrio, and several other jurists and theologians, who have acquired a sad notoriety as judges of witch-trials, in their writings ascribe the origin of witchcraft to Zoroaster.

The dualistic notion was not modified after entering Christianity, but intensified. The religion of Zoroaster, which presupposes a good first principle,* allows the evil which has in time arisen, in the course of time to disappear; and it ends with the doctrine which shines out faintly even in the New Testament, of the final "restoration of all things" (ἀποκατάστασις πάντων), and in consequence reduces evil to something merely phenomenal. In the doctrines of the Church, however, as they were established through the influence of Augustine, the Manicheian, evil, though arisen in time, is made eternal. This difference is of great practical significance and explains why dualism did not bear the same terrible fruits in its home in the Orient as in the Occident. The awful separation and contrast with which the divina comedia of the Middle Ages ends,—the wails and curses that arise from hell to intensify the

---

* This has been denied in so far as the original teachings of Zoroaster are concerned, but is confirmed by a passage in Aristotle (Metaphys., I., xiv., c. 4).

bliss of the redeemed,—form a conception so revolting that it could not be incorporated with thought and feeling without rendering them savage. Compassion, benevolence, love, —those qualities through which man feels a kinship with the divine, lose their significance and are despoiled of their eternal seal, when they are found no longer in his Maker except as limited or rather suspended by the action of another quality which the pious man will force himself to call justice, but which an irrepressible voice from the innermost recesses of his soul calls cruelty. To this must be added a further important consideration. The servant of Ormuzd is no more the property of the devil than the earth he treads upon. To be sure he is surrounded on every side by the treachery of Ahriman and all the demons, but this only because he is called and already endowed with power to be the champion of the Good upon the earth. It is as such that he is placed in the tumult of the battle. The power for good once imparted to him, and constantly renewed through prayer,

is withal also his own; he may use it without losing himself in the perplexing ques-
tion where liberty ceases and grace begins.
Every one adhering to the doctrine of light
stands on his own feet. This is true of every
servant of Ormuzd; Zoroaster has made in
this respect no distinction between priest and
layman. Even belief upon authority, in itself an encroachment upon free personality,
preserves for it in this form of religion a free
and inviolable arena.

In the Church of the Middle Ages the case
is different, and it cannot be presented better
than in the following words of the Neo-Lu-
theran Vilmar, when he would preserve absolutely to the clergy "the power to keep
the congregation together by the word, the
sacraments and ecclesiastical authority, the
power to cleave the head of sin with a single
word, the power to descend into a soul in
which the enemy has spread the gloom of
insanity and force the defiant knees of the
maniac to bend and his frenzied fists to fold
in prayer, yea, the power [here we have the

climax, which is rather tame after the fore-
going] to descend into a soul in which the
ancient enemy has established his abode, and
there fight the insolent giant from the realms
of darkness face to face and eye to eye. All
this"—continues Vilmar, himself not unlike
a frantic conjurer wishing to summon the
ghost of the Dark Ages from its grave—"all
this is not in the power of the congregation
nor of the ministry, who are not endowed
with the requisite authority, commission,
mandate and power. The congregation (*i. e.*,
the laymen) is not able to look into the furi-
ous eyes of the devil; for what is prophesied
of the last days, that even the elect, were
it possible, should be seduced, applies with
greater force to the especial apparition of Satan in this world: before it the congregation
is scattered like flakes of snow, not seduced
but terrified to death. Only we (the clergy)
are unterrified and fearless; for he who has
rejected the prince of this world has placed
us before the awful serpent-eye of the archfiend, before his blasphemous and scornful

4

mouth, before his infernally distorted face."*
These words from the pen of a fanatical du-
alist of our own time well represent, as in-
dicated above, the commonly received views
of the Middle Ages; and it is not therefore to
be wondered at that the mediæval generations, surrendering personality, threw themselves precipitately, in order to be saved, into
the arms of the magical institution of deliverance. The phenomena which are delineated
in the following pages will not seem so arbitrary and strange after this introductory
glance at the middle-age philosophy, as they
might otherwise at first sight. Even they are
a product of an inner necessity. Were it possible—and deplorable attempts are not want-
ing—to revive in the thoughts, feelings and
imagination of humanity the dogmas of mediæval times, we should then witness a partial
re-enactment of their terrible scenes. To de-
pict them has not only a purely historic inter-
est, but a cautionary and practical as well.

* A. F. Ch. Vilmar: "Theologie der Thatsachen wider die
Theologie der Rhetorik" (Marburg, 1857).

II.

THE MAGIC OF THE CHURCH.

Magic is the harbinger of Science. In the history of human development, the dim perception precedes the clear, and the dominion of imagination that of reason. Before the latter could take upon itself the laborious task of connecting together by its own laws the facts of external and internal experience,— before there was any philosophy or natural science, imagination was bestirring itself in the creation of magic.

Like science, magic in its original form is based upon the principle that all things existing are concatenated. Science searches for the links of union both deductively and inductively; magic, seeking its support in the external resemblances between existing things,* and in a vague assurance of the power of the will and of words, establishes this connection freely by means of arbitrary associations between incongruous objects. Man engaged in a struggle for physical existence, aims in it less at theoretical *knowing* than at practical *being able.* The knowledge of mysteries will furnish means of becoming acceptable to his God, inaccessible to injurious influences, and master of his present and future existence and destiny.

The magical usages which exist among every people, present an almost infinite variety of forms. In the end, however, they can all be reduced to a single type.

Daily experience has taught that there exists between every cause and its effect a certain proportionate amount of force. Now since the effect aimed at in resorting to magic is of an extraordinary nature, the means which the magical art prescribes must possess

---

* Thus, for instance, the red lustre of copper was supposed to indicate that it was connected with Mars, which shines with a reddish light.

extraordinary efficacy, such as reason can pre-
dict for it neither *a priori* nor by inductive
reasoning. Furthermore, experience teaches
us that will, as a mere inert desire, not yet
expressed in action, does not attain its goal.
Magical power therefore can not be sought
for in the mere will as such, but action, that
working of the senses which the will employs
as a means, in which it reveals itself, must be
added, whether the force of this sense-means,
as the original magic supposes, depends on
its mystical but necessary connection with its
corresponding object in a higher sphere (for
example, the connection between the metals
and the planets), or as in the Church-magic,
on an arbitrary decision of God, ordaining
that a given means, employed as prescribed
by him, shall produce an effect inconceivable
by reason. In all employment of magic enter consequently, first, the subjective spiritual factor,—the will (in the language of
the Church, faith); secondly, the sensuous
means,—the fetich, the amulet, the holy water, the host, the formula of exorcism, the

ceremony, etc.; and thirdly, the incomprehensible ("supernatural") power which this means, appropriated by the will (or faith), possesses in the magical act.

A belief in magic is found among all nations. With those of unitarian views it was destined to be forced more and more into the background by the growth of speculation and natural science. With them there was also but one form of magic, although those in possession of its secret were considered able to exercise it for a useful or an injurious purpose alike. Only among nations holding dualistic views do we meet with magic in two forms: with the priests a *white* and a *black*,— the former as the good gift of Ormuzd, the latter as the evil gift of Ahriman; with the Christians of the Middle Ages a *celestial* magic and a *diabolical*,—the former a privilege of the Church and conferred by God as a weapon to aid in the conquest of Satan; the latter an infernal art to further unbelief and wickedness. Under a unitarian theory magic is only a preparation for natural philosophy and gradually gives place to it, until it is confined to the lowest classes as a relic of a past stage of development. The dualistic religious systems, on the contrary, blend in an intimate union with magic, give to it the same universally and eternally valid power which they ascribe to themselves, and place it on their own throne in the form of a divine and sacramental secret. Only thus can faith in magic stamp whole ages and periods of culture with its peculiar seal; only thus—after its separation into celestial and diabolical, and in that causal relation to the temporal or eternal weal or woe of man in which it is placed— does it become possessed of an absolute sovereignty over the imagination and emotions of a people.

Our consideration of the middle-age magic may commence with a description of the celestial or privileged magic, that is to say, *that of the Church;* in order that we may proceed in natural order to the ill-reputed magic of the *learned* (astrology, alchemy, sorcery), and the persecuted *popular* magic (in which the

Church saw the really diabolical form); and end with an account of the terrible catastrophe which was caused by the contest which raged between them.

It is not the fault of the writer if the reader finds in the magic of the Church a caricature of what is holy, in which the comical element is overbalanced by the repulsive. The more objective the representation is to be made, the more unpleasant its features become. We will, then, be brief.

Like a thoughtful mother the Church cherishes and cares for man, and surrounds him from the cradle to the grave with its safeguards of magic. Shortly after the birth of a child the priest must be ready to sprinkle it with holy water, which by prayer and conjuration has been purified from the pollution of the demons inhabiting even this element. For the feeble being begotten in sin and by nature Lucifer's property, without the grace

This is the end of this publication.

Any remaining blank pages are for our book binding
requirements and are blank on purpose.

To search thousands of interesting publications like this one,
please remember to visit our website at:

http://www.kessinger.net

www.ingramcontent.com/pod-product-compliance
Lightning Source LLC
LaVergne TN
LVHW082142040326
832903LV00005B/253